THE STORY

YORK

by

Alan Avery

BLACKTHORN PRESS

Blackthorn Press, Blackthorn House
Middleton Rd, Pickering YO18 8AL
United Kingdom

ISBN 978 1 906259 01 3

© Alan Avery 2007

www.blackthornpress.com

2nd Edition 2008

Book design by Simon Ellis
Email: simon@flexibubbleart.co.uk

CONTENTS

ROMAN YORK

The story of York begins in 43 AD when the Roman Emperor Claudius ordered the invasion of the British Isles. By 70 AD the south of the Islands had been conquered and pacified and the Ninth Legion, under its commander Petilius Cerialis began its march north to conquer the rest of the new colony.

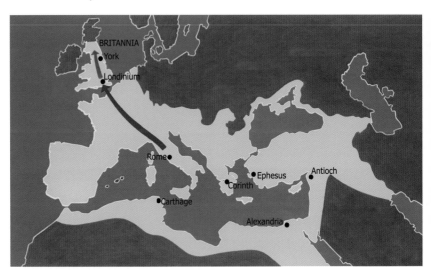

By 71 AD it had reached the area where York now stands and the officers and surveyors of the Legion began to scout for a suitable place to establish a fort as a place of safety in an unknown and hostile land and as a base for further conquest. The spot where the River Foss runs into the River Ouse was selected as a place offering some height above the surrounding countryside, safety on two sides provided by the rivers, with a supply of water and a connection to the sea via the rivers Ouse and Humber. A Roman Legionary pushed his spade into the earth to begin the construction of the ditch and bank and wooden palisade, typical of Roman forts, and the history of York began.

The Romans called the fort *Eboracum*, which could mean 'the place of the yews' and the surrounding inhabitants from the Celtic Brigante tribe, would have looked with curiosity and perhaps hostility and some wonder as the fort grew, towers and gateways were added and the sound of activity rang from within the walls. Forage parties would have left the fort to reconnoitre the surrounding country and perhaps bargain for or commandeer food and materials for the fort and its soldiers.

The plan of the fort was typical of most Roman forts being playing-card shaped with a gate in the centre of each side and the headquarters, or *Principia*, in the middle where the roads met. The rest of the space was given over to barracks and store-houses and the baths which were built of stone from the start.

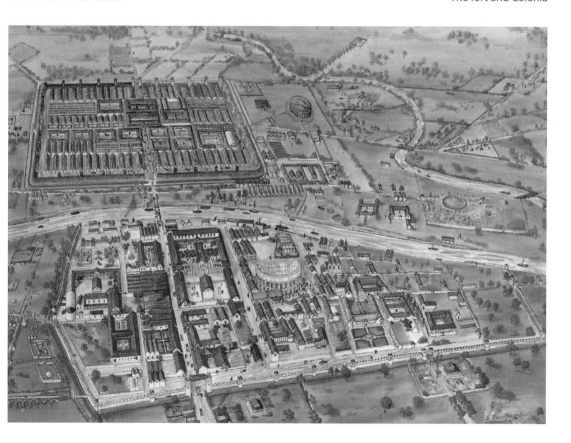

As well as the fort, the 5,000 soldiers of the legion would have been responsible for the building of the roads which radiated out from the fort, allowing good communications and the rapid deployment of troops wherever they were needed.

Outside the walls of the fort and later across the river another area, the *Colonia* or civilian area, began to grow. At first this would have been inhabited by the families of the soldiers and the camp followers who supplied the fort with its needs but over the years, the area grew to become a separate town with baths, an arena, market place, shops, as well as temples and shrines to the usual Roman Gods but also to Isis and Mithras a god of Persian origin popular with soldiers. A shrine to this god probably stood on Micklegate near St Martin Cum Gregory church where a relief to the God was found. At its peak, the population of the *Colonia* would have reached around 5,000 people and would have been connected to the fort by a bridge.

Below
Street scene in
Roman York

Archaeologists are discovering more about the life of the people who lived and worked in Roman York. We know very little about York from the written record but excavations have unearthed the stone foundations of many of the buildings and fortifications, which have enabled the historians to put together a plan of how the town was laid out. Apart from these large discoveries, many small items of everyday life have been found which give an insight into how the people of the fort and Colonia lived. These include coins, pots and glass and a host of objects made from other materials. In the area around modern Tanner Row, the boggy ground yielded materials used by the craftsmen of the time such as leather and iron tools and the remains of wooden buildings. One panel of an army tent had the name of a centurion, Sollius Julianus, scratched on it. His name later turned up on a building stone at Hadrian's Wall.

Left Location of the Roman Fort

Equally fascinating are the gravestones which have been unearthed, as the inscriptions on these give us the names and origins of the buried person. The gravestone of Lucius Duccius Rufinus, which can be seen in the Yorkshire Museum, tells us that he was a standard bearer and came from Vienne in the Rhone Valley while the gravestone of Julia Velva, an upper-crust lady, who died at the age of fifty, shows her surrounded by family and servants in a room in her house. Over the centuries, burial customs changed, with the slaves and poor being put in shallow graves, the rich in elaborate mausoleums and some being cremated and their ashes put in fascinating head pots. One Roman Emperor, Septimius Severus, died in York whilst campaigning in Britain and he was cremated with much ceremony before his ashes were shipped off to Rome.

Above Head pot found in York in the early third century

Right Tombstone of Julia Velva

The houses of the better-off would have had central heating and piped water with a fine view of the river while the working population lived in tenement blocks of less grandeur.

The Multangular Tower

Around about the year 150 AD, the wooden buildings and fortifications began to be replaced by stone. The work was largely done by the sixth legion, which had taken over from the ninth. One of the stone towers, the Multangular tower, which stood at the west corner of the fort can still be seen above ground in the museum gardens while other foundation stones have been excavated in recent years.

The main building of the fort was the *Principia* or Headquarters. Here were the administrative offices for the legion and a shrine to the most important Roman gods. This stood where the present Minster now stands and stone columns from the original building can be seen just outside the south entrance and in the crypt of the Minster. The main roads in the fort ran to and from the *Principia* and a walk along Petergate to Bootham Bar follows the Roman road, *via principalis*. The Medieval Bootham Bar sits on top of one of the original Roman gateways to the fort. As well as the foundations of the walls and the Principia, those of houses, baths, store-rooms and roads have also been found.

Right
The main bath sewer

Perhaps the most exciting discovery was the main baths sewer which lies under modern Church Street. It is nearly 1½ metres high and made of massive blocks of stone. Water to flush the sewer may even have been piped in from as far away as Malton, some 20 kilometres from York.

York's status was further increased when Britain was divided into two provinces in 237 AD and York was chosen as the capital of the Northern Province and London that of the Southern. This would have meant further officials and their families increasing the demand for goods and accommodation.

Over the 340 years of Roman York's existence, its wealth and status would have fluctuated with the vagaries and often turbulent politics of the Empire but by 410 A.D. Rome could no longer maintain the legions in Britain as the Germanic tribes pressed on Rome itself and the Legions were withdrawn leaving Britain to defend itself. With the withdrawal of the troops and their families, York became a shadow of its former self. Roads became disused, rubbish piled up in the streets, houses fell into decay and the bridge across the river collapsed. The defences and roads remained and whoever was to fill the vacuum left by the end of Roman rule, could not ignore these.

Constantine

In the year 306, the Emperor Constantinius I died in York while campaigning in this country. It was expected that Flavius Severus would succeed him but the all-powerful army preferred his son Constantine and they proclaimed him Emperor in York. It is not certain that Constantine was in York to hear the proclamation but a large statue was raised to him, the head being found in Stonegate in the 19th century. Constantine is largely remembered as being the first Roman Emperor to allow Christians to worship freely in the Empire and a modern statue to him was placed outside the Minster.

Constantine

CONSTA

ANGLO-SAXON AND VIKING YORK

In the six hundred and fifty-six years which separated the withdrawal of the Roman legion from York in 410 to the arrival of the Normans in 1066, York changed from an almost deserted city to be the capital of a Viking kingdom and the second city in the country after London.

We know very little of the period immediately after the Roman withdrawal. The city may well have been deserted, the local Britons drifting back to the countryside to make a living although it has been suggested that some form of local government could have survived, centred on the old Roman headquarters. There is no written record and very little archaeological evidence to tell us how the impoverished inhabitants of York organised themselves. Certainly, all traces of Roman goods disappeared as the citizens reverted to products made of local materials.

The Angles and Saxons from present day Germany had been raiding the Yorkshire coast while the Romans were present and once they had gone the raiders came to conquer and then to settle. Present day Yorkshire was settled by the Angles who founded the kingdom of Deira. Two cemeteries with Anglo-Saxon urns have been discovered just outside York, which suggest that the Anglo-Saxons had reached the city by the late fifth century.

In 597 Pope Gregory sent Augustine and a band of monks to the heathen Saxons who had settled the south of England. Thanks to the help of King Ethelbert's wife, Berta who was already a Christian, Augustine was able to establish the first Roman Catholic churches in the south.

The first Anglian king we know of is Aella who reigned from 560 A.D. By 625 Aella's son Edwin was king not only of Deira but the whole of Northumbria. He married King Ethelbert's daughter, Ethelburga, who like her mother was a Christian. Ethelburga persuaded her new husband to allow one of Augustine's monks, Paulinus to preach the new religion and, despite some reservations, Edwin himself was baptised on Easter day 627 in a little wooden church which was quickly constructed in York. This church was to be the first of many constructions culminating in the York Minster we know today. Paulinus became the first of a long line of bishops based at the new church. There is no evidence that the kings of Deira used York as a capital city. The rebuilding of the new church in stone was abandoned with the death in battle of Edwin in 633 and the new king, Oswald, shifted the centre of power northwards to Bamburgh. Lindisfarne was chosen as the new seat of the bishop. However, by 644 the bishopric was back in York.

Below
Paulinus preaches
to Edwin

In 735 the Bishop of York was made an Archbishop and gradually Edwin's original church was improved with stone replacing wood and a new lead roof and glazed windows but all was lost in a fire in 741. After that date the exact location of the church is unclear. It is even suggested that it moved across the river within the old civilian town.

Below
The Occupation of
York in 850 AD

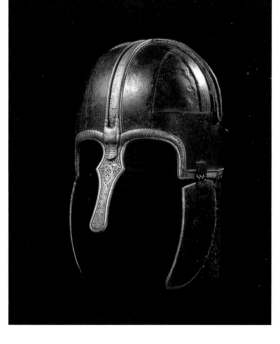

For two hundred years Christianity in England was centred on Yorkshire with churches and monasteries such as Whitby acting as centres of learning and conversion. Missionaries were sent out to heathen Europe to make conversions to the new faith. In York a library and school was established which became internationally famous in the 8th and 9th centuries. Its greatest scholar Alcuin made a centre of learning in York which was seen as second only to Rome and Alcuin himself travelled to Europe in the 780s and became part of Charlemagne's court.

Because it was the priests and monks who were literate we know a good deal about the history of the church but everyday life in York at this time is less clear.

Below
Anglian Warrior's
Helmet

How long the stone structures of Roman York lasted we do not know. Many may have simply fallen with the passage of time and others were deliberately dismantled and their foundations used to support wooden structures. Certainly, the grid pattern of the Roman roads gave way to diagonal paths which criss-crossed the city. We do not have any evidence for buildings of the 7th to 9th century although artefacts from the period have been found. Coins bearing the names of Anglian kings and the Archbishop of York have been found which suggests a mint in the city. Metal, jewellery and a little pottery have turned up but certainly the most magnificent find from Anglian York is the warrior's helmet which for reason unknown was buried in the city.

The Anglians called York 'Eoforwic' which suggests that the city had become a centre of trade as well as a royal enclave centred on the defences of the old Roman fort. Certainly, continental pottery has been found and a continental writer mentions a colony of Frisian merchants based in or near York. Archaeologists have found evidence for habitation and manufacturing going on from around 700 to 850 in Fishergate where the rivers Ouse and Foss meet. It could then be that York had established itself as a centre for the manufacture of luxury goods for local aristocrats or for exchange for foreign goods.

VIKING YORK

In the year 787, the Anglo-Saxon chronicle or history recorded, 'In this year, King Beorhtric of Wessex took to wife Eadburh, daughter of King Offa. And in his days came first three ships of Norsemen from Hörthaland: and the reeve rode thither and tried to compel them to go to the royal manor, for he did not know what they were: and they slew him'.

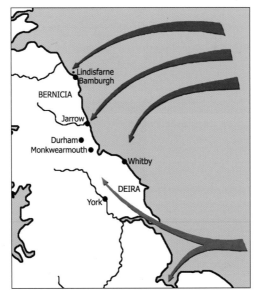

Right
The Viking Raids

At first the Vikings from Scandinavia looted easy targets on the coast such as the monastery at Lindisfarne in 793 but over the years they became bolder and in 865 a Danish army led by Ivar the Boneless, landed in East Anglia, marched northward and in 866 captured York. With typical Viking cunning they attacked on All Saints Day, knowing that the city's key figures would be at worship in the Cathedral and could probably be captured for ransom. Two Northumbrian kings present, Aelle and Osberht, escaped and the Vikings moved on to campaign around the Tyne. They returned to York the following year and this time Aelle and Osberht were killed in the ensuing battle.

Present day Yorkshire follows largely the boundaries settled by the Vikings as they moved in to the surrounding countryside and their organisation of the county into 'Trithings' or thirds, continued in the three 'Ridings' until the twentieth century.

The new Viking kingdom of York lasted from 875 until 954 with more than a dozen Norse kings from Halfdan to Eric Bloodaxe who lost it in 954, slain in battle by the Wessex King Edred.

From then on York came under the sway of English and Danish kings, the most famous being Canute of Denmark who did much to unite his English and Danish subjects under one code of law.

York was again at the centre of England's history in the year 1066. Harold Godwinson was king but his crown was claimed by Harold Hardrada of Norway and Duke William of Normandy. The first to strike was Hardrada. Amassing a huge fleet of 300 long boats he sailed along the Yorkshire coast, landing at various locations, including Scarborough, which he burned to the ground when the inhabitants refused to open their gates. Finally, he sailed up the rivers Humber and the Ouse to Riccall and from there marched on York. An army under Edwin and Morcar met the Norwegians at Fulford and were defeated by Hardrada who then camped at Stamford Bridge to await the arrival of Harold Godwinson.

Harold arrived on the 25th of September and faced the Norwegian army. Hardrada claimed the throne of England but all Godwinson would grant him was 'seven feet, enough for a grave, or since he was a tall man perhaps a little more'. This promise was fulfilled as the Norwegians and their allies, which included Godwinson's own brother Tostig, were slain wholesale, the few survivors managing to reach their boats and sail away. The king and his army marched into York to celebrate their victory.

Above
King Canute and Queen Emma present an alter cross to New Minster, 1031

The celebrations were cut short by the news that Duke William of Normandy had landed on the south coast and was burning and looting and defying Harold to meet him in battle. Harold gathered his forces and marched the 180 miles to Hastings were he died surrounded by his bodyguard, the last Anglo-Saxon king.

Thanks to the work of archaeologists, we know much of what life was like in Viking York or 'Jorvik' as it was then known. A trip to York's Jorvik Museum will bring the sites and smells of the city to life for the visitor.

Excavations around the Coppergate area and at other sites in York have uncovered a number of dwelling houses which appear to have been combined with workshops. These structures are known as 'cellared buildings', having a cellar dug out of the ground which was then lined with substantial trunks before the main building was added.

Below

An impression of how a late tenth-century basemented building was constructed.

The quantity and quality of the objects found in Viking York point to mass production by specialist workers. Pottery spun on a wheel and wooden objects turned on a lathe have been found as well as a variety of goods made of copper, iron, wood and leather. York was the only town north of the Humber and was able to draw on the raw materials from a wide area and to sell back the finished goods to this area and probably even overseas. Goods of foreign manufacture have been found in York, ranging from walrus ivory from the far north to silk from Istanbul and no doubt ships unloading these goods looked for items manufactured in York to take back with them.

Below Jorvik 975 A.D.

The period of relative peace, which followed the end of Viking rule, saw the establishment of many of York's parish churches, largely by wealthy individuals. At least fifteen churches were established in York before the Norman invasion of 1066, amongst them St Andrew, Fishergate. Much of the old Roman walls were still standing, in places as high as fourteen feet, and where they were lacking, wooden palisades were added and even new walls built to plug gaps in the defences.

Above St Andrew's Church - A pre Norman Church

An impression of how York's earlier defences were reused and refurbished in the Viking Age

Everywhere are signs of activity and expansion as York grew in size and importance. English and Danish kings appointed an Earl of Northumbria to run their northern territories and he was based in York which still maintained the feel and sounds of a Scandinavian city. Many of the streets in York are called 'gates' from the Danish word for street, 'gade' and the surrounding countryside is full of villages with Danish names. In The Life of St Oswald written about 1000 A.D. is the following description of York:

Above Street name

'The city of York is the capital of the whole people of the Northumbrians…The city rejoices in the multitude of its population, which counting men and women but not infants and children, numbers not less than 30,000. The city is crammed beyond expression, and enriched with treasures of merchants, who come from all parts, but above all from the Danish people'.

Tostig

At the church of Kirkdale, some twenty miles north of York a sundial is set into the wall bearing the inscription 'Orm, the son of Gamal, bought St Gregory's church when it was all broken and fallen, and caused it to be made anew from the ground for Christ and St Gregory in the days of King Edward, and in the days of Earl Tostig …'

This was the same Earl Tostig who was to die at the battle of Stamford Bridge, fighting against his brother Harold. Even by the harsh standards of the day, Tostig was brutal beyond reason. As the king's brother he was entrusted with the running of England north of the Humber with his base in York but his behaviour was so cruel, including the murder of Gamal, the restorer of Kirkdale church, that he was banished by the king in 1065. He promptly fled to Norway and offered his services to the Norwegian King Hardrada. He sailed with the Norwegian fleet which attacked York in 1066 and died at the battle of Stamford Bridge.

YORK IN THE MIDDLE AGES

The Middle Ages in England begins with the arrival of Duke William of Normandy in 1066 and ends with the defeat of Richard III at the battle of Bosworth in 1485. During that time York went from despair and destruction to what has been called the 'Halcyon Years', when the city rose to a glory symbolised by its beautiful Minster.

William quickly took control of the south of England after his coronation in London by Aldred, the Archbishop of York. The north would be a different matter. Although of Danish origin, the Normans had adopted the language and customs of their French neighbours and were seen as unwanted foreigners by the citizens of York who were still largely of Scandinavian origin.

Below
The first Norman Castle

William and his army arrived in York in 1086 facing a rebellion by the Earls Edwin and Morcar. The king quickly built two wooden castles and left it with a garrison under the sheriff, William Malet. But as soon as the king left, the inhabitants rebelled and stormed the castles, burning them to the ground, forcing the king to return and sack the town, burning many buildings and killing hundreds of its inhabitants. The forts were rebuilt but in 1069 a Danish fleet led by King Swein arrived in York and slew 3,000 Normans. William was quick to avenge this insult returning to York again only to find the Danes had left. This did not stop him wreaking terrible revenge in the whole of northern England in what has been called the 'Harrying of the North' when towns and villages were burned and thousands massacred.

Following this setback, York accepted Norman rule and began the slow climb back to prosperity and pre-eminence as the capital of the north and second city after London.

A huge programme of public building began in York including the two castles, which spanned the river, churches, walls with their 'bars' or gates, St Mary's Abbey with its King's Manor, the monastery of Holy Trinity, St Leonard's Hospital and a Minster in the new Norman style. A dam was built across the river Foss creating marsh land which protected one side of the city and gave the inhabitants a good supply of fish.

Below
The Norman Minster

The Minster church we see today is the result of much adding and modification over the centuries. The present Minster is perhaps the sixth on the site. The first Norman Archbishop, Thomas of Bayeux, had a Minster built in the style of the church in Bayeux but a later Archbishop, Walter de Gray, began the demolition of this building in 1241 and the building of the present south transept began. By the time of Walter's death in 1255 the north transept and the Five Sisters window were in place. In 1400 the Norman church had all but disappeared and the Minster had taken on its present interior structure. By 1472 the towers and exterior decorations were completed and the Minster, free of scaffolding, was seen as one of the architectural glories of Europe.

Above York Minster

At the time of the Norman conquest, the population of York was probably around 8,000 most of whom lived within the walls of the city. A steady growth took place, despite the ravages of the Black Death, until by 1400 it was about 15,000. Conditions within the walls for the ordinary citizens were squalid with narrow streets and open sewers but with more stable times, the city began to spread outside its walls alongside the roads which led out of the gates.

Right The Shambles

York Minster

As the Norman influence moved north, the main threat was from Scotland. The Scots frequently came over the disputed border and in 1138 the Scottish army reached within thirty miles of York. The Archbishop of York, Thurstan, rallied the people of York and the local nobility to counter the threat and their army faced the Scots outside Northallerton, where they inflicted a crushing defeat at the so-called 'Battle of the Standard'.

Later in the twelfth century an event took place, which shook and shamed York. Anti-Jewish feeling was rife throughout the country and in 1190 mobs in York began to attack Jews and their property. The Jewish community sought shelter and protection in the castle where the mob began to lay siege. Rather than fall into their hands, the Jewish rabbi Yomtob, suggested they commit suicide and he began by cutting the throats of his wife and sons. The next morning, the few survivors were massacred by the mob. This was no spontaneous uprising, for the nobles involved were careful to make sure that the documents relating to loans from the Jews were burned in the Minster and the authorities did nothing to protect the Jews. Only when law and order was restored by King **Below** Clifford's Tower Richard I, did the leaders flee the country or suffer heavy fines.

The church was one of the most powerful influences in York. Despite having given way to the Archbishop of Canterbury as the leader of the Church in England, the presence of an Archbishop in York did much to enhance the wealth and prestige of the city. In addition to the Minster, York housed two Benedictine monasteries, St Mary's Abbey being the largest in the north of England. There was also a house of Gilbertine monks at St Andrew's Fishergate and Clementhorpe Nunnery. The four orders of Friars later settled in York and established their houses and finally there were about forty parish churches scattered throughout the city. All of these establishments brought employment, wealth and prestige to the city.

The king was represented in the city by the sheriff. The office goes back to Anglo-Saxon times but was adopted and adapted by the Normans. The sheriff's duties were the collection of taxes, keeping the peace and administering justice as well as organising local defences. The first sheriff whose name we have is Gamel, 1066-1068 and the office has continued to this day.

York contained many powerful families such as the Selbys and Tickhills who over the years banded together in a Council to promote their own interests and incidentally the interests of the City against the crown and the church. Around 1156, Henry II granted York its first Royal charter setting the laws and liberties of the citizens of York. A further charter granted by King John in 1212, allowed the title of Mayor and the first known Mayor was Hugh Selby, appointed by the Council in 1217. Since 1396 the city virtually administered its own affairs and from the time of Henry VI it also spread its influence to govern a stretch of land outside the city, known as the Ainsty, between the rivers Wharfe, Nidd and Ouse.

Crown, Church and Council vied for influence in York, not always peacefully or legally. In 1260 the city was placed under papal interdict because the Mayor had hanged a lady called Annabella whom the Chapter of the Minster had claimed the right of hanging in their own court. In 1264 St Mary's Abbey was driven to build a high wall around itself to protect itself from the citizens who looted the grounds and attacked anyone who got in their way.

The crowded streets were home to many trades: weavers, glovers, saddlers, hosiers, butchers, drapers and vintners all organised themselves

into Guilds trading from the busy port of York. Modern street names come from these times with Coppergate being the coopers districts and Spurriergate where the spur makers had their shops. Ship building was an important part of the local economy with 69 shipwrights being recorded in the city in 1296, more than anywhere else in the kingdom, including London which had only 50. The annual fair and weekly markets brought the countryside to town with fresh produce in exchange for

Above Street Market

manufactured goods and cash. York merchants were known throughout Europe, trading in cloth and fine manufactured goods and it was largely these wealthy merchants who formed the city Council, built the Guildhall and Merchant Adventurers' Hall and patronised the arts such as the cycle of mystery plays and the building of churches and chapels replete with statues and stained glass.

Right Merchant Venturers' Hall

1272 is seen as a turning point in the History of York. The new king, Edward I, involved himself with wars against the Welsh, Irish and French but more importantly for York, the Scots. The king needed to be near the border and used York as his northern base, turning the city into almost a second capital. In return for further taxes to finance the wars, the Council exacted further privileges from the crown until it virtually ran its own affairs. Money flowed into the merchants' coffers as the demand for men and materiel to fight the wars seemed insatiable. Not that the monarchs' wars were always advantageous for the city. Edward II's disastrous campaigns meant the Scots were free to roam the north of England and in 1319 a Scots army appeared in the Vale of York. A motley army marched out of the city to take on the Scots near Boroughbridge and were duly annihilated, including the then Mayor, Nicholas Flemnyng. In 1322 the Scots reached York and terrorised the suburbs but the walls of the city deterred a full-scale attack.

Left Mickelgate Bar

Edward III moved his court to York in 1328, married his queen in the Minster and called no fewer than fifteen Parliaments to the city. But this was to be the high point of York's political and military influence. The young king had his eyes on a greater prize than Scotland – the throne of France – and the campaign known as the Hundred Years War effectively moved the centre of influence back to London where it has remained.

Medieval kings continued to visit the city. Richard II particularly favoured it and he is recorded as watching the mystery plays with great pleasure. Henry IV fined York £200 and had Archbishop Scrope executed for daring to oppose him. During the Wars of the Roses, 1455-1485, York was used by both sides as a base and as a place to hang the heads of slain enemies, 'Off with his head, and set it on York gates; So York may overlook the town of York' *(Shakespeare's King Henry VI)* but took no active part in the fighting.

Below Mystery Play

The last years of the Middle Ages were ones of relative decline for York. The moving of the court back to London, the turmoil of the Wars of the Roses, the ravages of the Black Death and the growing competition for York's trade from the new port of Hull and the Hanseatic League meant the glory days were over. It would take York many years to adapt to being a regional rather than a national centre.

William FitzHerbert

No Medieval town or city felt itself complete without its own saint. They were a status symbol, a centre of religious faith in a time when religion and preparation for the next life dominated men's thoughts and an attraction to draw pilgrims to the city. Canterbury had Thomas Becket and Beverley St John. York's choice fell on one of its Archbishops, William FitzHerbert. William was a popular local man who was first elected Archbishop in 1143 but had to give up the position and flee abroad following opposition from the Pope and powerful local enemies. In 1153, with his enemies all dead, William returned to York to reclaim his throne. Such was the crowd that turned out to greet him that the bridge over the Ouse collapsed under their weight but 'miraculously' no one was drowned. Further miracles were said to have occurred around William and on his death he was made a saint complete with a splendid tomb. But for a few fragments, the tomb is lost but the miracle of the Ouse bridge and other miracles are there for all to see in the stained glass of the Minster's St William's window.

TUDOR YORK

When Henry VII lifted the crown of England on to his head at the Battle of Bosworth in 1485 to be the first Tudor monarch, York found itself in a difficult position. It had openly supported Richard III and had expected much from him as a local magnate.

Indeed, York was suffering economically. Many of the weavers and merchants had moved out of the city to the West Riding where costs were lower and the stranglehold of the Guilds could be avoided. The population was falling, reaching 8,000 by 1550 and houses stood empty unable to find tenants at any rent. The Council had to repeatedly ask London for a reduction in its taxes being unable to pay the high levels assessed when York was flourishing.

So when Henry visited York in 1486 the Council pulled out all the stops to make him welcome with pageants and vows of loyalty. The next year a revolt against Henry was led by Lambert Simnel, a baker's son who pretended to be of royal blood but the City remained loyal being

Below Henry VIII

rewarded by another royal visit and a special performance of the Mystery Plays which the king watched from Thomas Scott's house in Coney Street.

The Council seemed to be having trouble maintaining law and order with elements of the commons resorting to violence to preserve their perceived rights. The new king, Henry VIII revoked the city's old charters issuing a new one in 1517 which virtually removed all the powers of the commoners who until then had nominated the Mayor and placed control almost exclusively in the hands of the ruling merchant elite.

St Mary's Ruins

Henry's interference in York's affairs continued as he sought revenues to carry out his foreign wars and his eyes turned to the wealth of the church. At first Henry confiscated only minor religious houses and in 1536 Clementhorpe Nunnery and Holy Trinity Priory were seized by the crown.

Later, however, Henry turned his attention to the larger religious houses and in York many religious houses surrendered or were seized. The summit was reached in the closure and selling off of St Mary's Abbey and St Leonard's Hospital in 1539. This was a serious blow to York which gained much revenue by servicing the churches and monasteries and benefited from their ministering and education. With the closing of St Leonard's Hospital and its two hundred beds, the sick of York were largely abandoned. Their roofs stripped of lead, many of the buildings fell into ruin, their stone being used to repair the churches that remained. Many of the clergy were absorbed into the parish churches or sought positions outside the city whilst others retired quietly on the pensions the luckier ones had been allotted.

These impositions of central government on the country did not go unopposed and in 1536 a rising started in nearby Beverley led by the lawyer, Thomas Aske, known as the 'Pilgrimage of Grace'. The 'pilgrims' wanted the restoration of the monasteries and religious houses but in an age which found it difficult to distinguish between religion and politics, Henry saw it as a threat to his throne and after promising the pilgrims what they wanted, quickly rounded up and hanged the leaders, Aske himself being executed at Clifford's Tower in York. York had allowed the pilgrims into the city and entertained many of them and although not active in the rebellion had incurred Henry's suspicion.

One result of this was the reintroduction of the Council in the North which Henry set up again in 1538 and which settled permanently in York in 1561 at the King's Manor, with Robert Holgate as its first president. The Council was virtually the legal and civic arm of the crown in the north of England from the Humber to the Scottish border and York was to benefit from its presence until the middle of the seventeenth century. With the Council officials and the stream of people from all over the north coming to use the legal and civic services, the demand for accommodation, food and labour soared with sixty-four inns being established by 1596. The population of York rose slowly but steadily to some 12,000 in 1600 fed largely by the poor of the countryside drifting into the city looking for work. Some succeeded but others ended in the newly established workhouse or 'house of correction'.

Left King's Manor Doorway

Henry died in 1547 and was succeeded by his young son Edward VI. Now began the see-saw of religious change from Edward's Protestantism to his sister Mary's devout Catholicism and then back to the Protestantism of Elizabeth I. Most bent with the wind of change, adopting the alterations, such as the removal of statues and the white-washing of churches to the more complex changes in ideologies which must have baffled all but the learned. Some were made of sterner stuff and refused to compromise. In York, thirty Catholic women were imprisoned in York Castle where over a third died. Margaret Clitherow was pressed to death in the York Tollbooth in 1586 for refusing to renounce her religion and in 1595 thirty Catholic priests were executed on the Knavesmire outside York.

By the end of Elizabeth's reign the new Protestant religion had taken root and was associated with loyalty to the crown whilst Catholicism was increasingly seen as 'foreign' or the religion of traitors.

York was thriving by the end of Elizabeth's reign having cleared all its civic debts, having three times the overseas trade of Hull and even able to build a new bridge over the Ouse in 1565 when the old medieval structure was swept away by floods. With the death of Elizabeth in 1603, the city looked with confidence to the arrival of her nephew King James I from Scotland to be James VI of England.

Right
The Old Ouse Bridge

Archbishop Robert Holgate

The life of Robert Holgate exemplifies the difficulties that men in public service faced with the constantly changing religious and political doctrines.

Holgate rose from obscurity to be Bishop of Llandaff and became a favourite at court. He was rewarded by being made President of the Council in the North and then the first protestant Archbishop of York in 1545. He rigorously applied the new doctrines of Edward VI, even at the age of sixty-eight, marrying a local gentlewoman, Barbara Wentworth to show that he supported the new doctrine of allowing priests to marry. When Mary came to the throne in 1553, the pendulum swung back to Catholicism and Holgate was despatched to the Tower of London. By renouncing his marriage and paying the enormous fine of £1000, he regained his freedom and returned to the Catholic faith living out his final days as a Catholic priest in London. He died in 1555, three years before Elizabeth came to the throne and the pendulum swung back to Protestantism.

STUART YORK

The new reign began well for York with James stopping in the city on his way south to London but euphoria gave way to despair when the plague struck York in the summer of 1604. Despite the attempts of the council to restrict movement in and out of the city, over one third of the population died before the last plague burial took place in April 1605. Remarkably, the city quickly recovered with new arrivals from the surrounding countryside taking advantage of the cheap housing and job opportunities. As ever, York remained the regional capital, at the hub of a distribution network which covered most of the north of England as well as being the legal and ecclesiastical focus for the north.

Below
Speed's map of
York in 1610

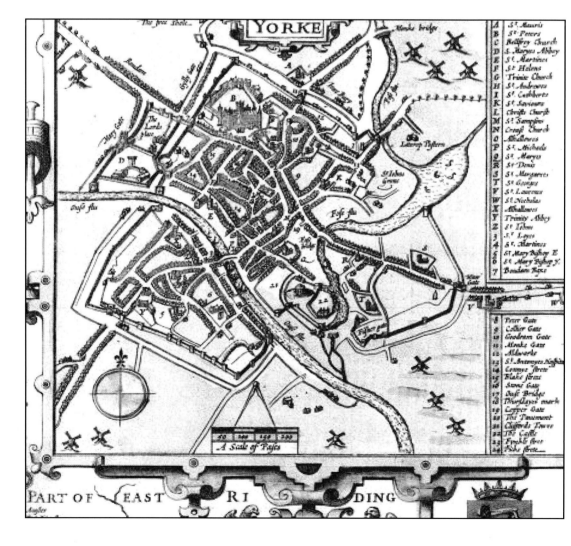

The distribution of Yorkshire cloth was still the main source of income but the supply of food and drink and accommodation and the growing number of skilled craftsmen such as bookbinders and clockmakers were to continue to increase throughout the seventeenth century. Growth was steady, if not spectacular, the population reaching 12,400 by 1700.

The city government continued to be in the hands of relatively few families, largely drawn from the merchant class and often related by blood or marriage. At the other end of the social scale, the many poor people of York relied on the charity of the rich who gave donations of food or money or built almshouses like those, which still stand in Bootham, built by Sir Arthur Ingram to house ten poor widows.

Above The plague strikes York in 1604

York played little part in national politics for the first forty years of the century apart from Guy Fawkes, the son of a York lawyer and educated at St Peter's School in York, who famously took part in the 1605 Gunpowder plot. Pupils at St Peter's School still do not place a 'Guy' on their bonfire, considering it 'bad form to burn an old boy'.

The religious life of the city largely mirrored the national picture. The national church had moved to the right with an insistence on the use of the Book of Common Prayer and orders to 'beautify' churches whilst many in the congregations were more Puritan minded preferring sermons and simple churches. In York, successive Archbishops tried to enforce their ideas whilst the City Council supported those Puritan clergy who resisted, paying for Puritan preachers and even buying the livings of two York churches, All Saints Pavement and St Saviour, so that they could appoint their own clergy.

Below Guy Fawkes

Charles I was strongly influenced by his Catholic wife and when visiting York in 1633 he granted the Minster authorities £1000 to set up an organ, to gild and colour the altar screen and to provide new plate and altar cloths.

Not only did the corporation and Minster disagree on matters of religion but also on who ran the city. The Minster still had extensive privileges over sizeable areas of York where tradesmen could avoid the council's regulations and petty criminals could escape the magistrates by living there.

The tensions between King and subjects in London grew as did Charles' deteriorating relationship with his Scottish subjects. Charles was in York in 1640 and 1641 preparing his army to fight the Scots and thousands of his troops were stationed on Clifton Ings and Bishop Fields. The failure of this campaign brought the council of Peers to York to arrange the resultant truce and to recall Parliament in London. These were the beginnings of the Civil War in which York was to play a crucial role.

Relations between King and Parliament in London deteriorated to such an extent that Charles fled the capital in March 1642 and moved his family and court to York making it, in effect, the capital of England. There were many who turned out to welcome the king but others were more on the side of Parliament. Samuel Wintour, rector of St Michael Spurriergate, preached a sermon praising Parliament as 'the assembly of God.' York seemed to be holding its breath, hoping for a peaceful settlement. The king left York on the 16 August for Nottingham leaving a garrison of 4,000 soldiers under the Duke of Newcastle. At Nottingham the king raised his standard, declaring the opening of hostilities between himself and Parliament and the beginning of the civil war, which would only end with the king's execution in 1649.

The military campaign came close to York in 1644 when the garrison marched to Selby and suffered a heavy defeat at the hands of Fairfax, a Yorkshire general. By the end of April York was surrounded by a Parliamentary army 20,000 strong. By June the besieging armies began bombarding the city and most of the suburbs outside the walls were burned down. The situation was desperate but on the 1st of July a relieving army under the king's nephew, Prince Rupert, cleverly manoeuvred its way into the city. The Duke of Newcastle was for delay but the impetuous Rupert led his troops out of the city to face the Parliamentary armies at Marston Moor. Here he suffered a bloody defeat with Oliver Cromwell's well disciplined cavalry being a major factor. Rupert and Newcastle fled and York surrendered shortly afterwards becoming from now on a Parliamentary stronghold.

The surrender
of York to the
Parliamentarians
after Marston Moor

The puritans now took control of affairs in York, dominating the council and removing many of the decorations from York's churches. Even the stained glass in the Minster was threatened but this was saved by Fairfax. The Council in the North, seen as a symbol of royal power and interference was abolished. However, national affairs could not be forgotten and when the Scots demanded a ransom of £20,000 for Charles, who had surrendered to them in 1646, it was counted out in the inner council chamber behind the Guildhall.

York settled down to recover and rebuild and despite disagreements within the council, welcomed the new king, Charles II, in 1660 once it was clear that the rule of the Commonwealth was over.

The Anglican Church was now in the ascendancy and many Puritan clergy and councillors were removed. Despite this, the presence of nonconformists was strong in York with Presbyterians, Independents, Baptists and Quakers all active in the city. Catholics continued to be persecuted and the gallows on the Knavesmire were again in use including the execution of Oliver Postgate a priest in his eighties who for fifty years had been serving the Catholic communities of the North Yorkshire Moors.

The hatred of Catholics came to a head in York in 1688 after the King's Catholic brother, James had come to the throne. The supporters of the Protestants William and Mary overpowered the garrison and seized the weapons store and in 1689 the corporation sent a message of congratulation to William once he and his wife had accepted the throne.

By the end of the seventeenth century York again took up its role as provider of craftsmen and leisure for a wide geographic area. There was horse-racing, coffee houses and an assembly room at the old King's Manor. Fashion was all and with it came dancing masters, wigmakers and booksellers. Artists and musicians settled in the city making it the cultural centre of the north. Many of its merchants and shopkeepers enriched themselves on the new colonial trade and employed builders and craftsmen in silver and glass to extend and adorn their properties. Many York craftsmen gained national reputations such as the glasspainter Henry Gyles whose work can not only be seen in York but in Ripon Minster, University College Oxford and in churches throughout the north.

Despite the new affluence for some, many remained desperately poor. Forty percent of the households in the Walmgate Ward were considered too poor to pay the hearth tax in 1672 and unemployment and illness were a daily threat for many. There was no great fire as in London to sweep away the old alleys and narrow streets and southern visitors to York such as Celia Fiennes thought the city made 'a meane appearance, the streetes are narrow and not of any length… the houses are very low and as indifferent as in any Country town.' But behind the apparent backwardness, York was thriving and the next century was to see the transformation of its physical appearance.

Below Water Lane

Thomas Fairfax

Thomas Fairfax was born in Denton in Yorkshire in 1612. At the age of seventeen he was in Holland learning to be a soldier and at the outbreak of the civil war his skills were put at the service of Parliament. He was made General of the Parliamentary cavalry and served with distinction at the battles of Marston Moor and Naseby. In 1650 he was ordered to march against the Scots who had declared Charles II king but he refused and retired into private life. With the death of Cromwell he was head of the commission sent to the Hague in 1660 to arrange for the return of Charles II. He died in 1671. Fairfax House in York is a fine example of a Georgian townhouse built by the Fairfax family.

YORK IN THE EIGHTEENTH CENTURY

There is no doubt that the loss of the King's Council in the North in 1641 was a blow to York's prestige and economy but it was still the seat of the Archbishop, the county town of Yorkshire, a garrison city and the place of business and pleasure for the northern aristocracy.

The presence of the military in York was a source of income for many although it saw little action during the troubled times of the Jacobite risings when supporters of the Stuarts invaded England, although a group of local gentry who had formed the Royal Regiment of Hunters engaged with the rebel army near Penrith. The Duke of Cumberland did pass through York on his way to Culloden and in 1745 the heads of two rebels were spiked on Micklegate.

Although York was the seat of the Archbishop, the Anglican church in York was in a poor state, perhaps as a reaction to the excesses of the previous century. Only the east end of the Minster was in use and by 1825 communion was only celebrated monthly because there were so few attending. At the remaining 24 parish churches livings were poor for the clergy and they often complained that parishioners were not enthusiastic about attending services.

Despite all the persecution they had suffered, Catholics held firm to their faith and by 1764 there were 82 Catholic families in York with their own chapel in Little Blake Street. John and Charles Wesley both preached in York but the number of Methodists were to remain small until the nineteenth century. The Quakers continued to grow in numbers and built their own Meeting House in Friargate in 1718. Presbyterians had their own chapel in St Saviourgate as early as 1692.

It was the use of York as a place of assembly and leisure by the cream of northern aristocrats such as the Duke of Rutland, Lord Carlisle and Lord Burlington which transformed York in the eighteenth century. Not only did these grandees build themselves fine houses such as Micklegate House, owned by Sir John Bourchier but they were instrumental in encouraging and often financing the range of public buildings which began to adorn York. The area of Castle Yard around Clifford's Tower took its present shape with new courthouses and prisons. Here the infamous highwayman Dick Turpin was tried and condemned to death and William Wilberforce addressed electors in the Castle Yard on the abolition of slavery. An Assembly Room designed by the Earl of Burlington was first used during Race Week in 1732 and a new stand was built at the racecourse on the Knavesmire. The Corporation decided that its Lord Mayor needed an official residence and in 1733 the then Lord Mayor, John Stainforth, moved into the magnificent Mansion House built in the Palladian style. The architect of the building has, strangely, never been discovered. The Theatre Royal was established in 1734 and attracted the best-known actors of the day.

Below Red House A Georgian House built for Sir William Robinson

Not that all the new building was done by the landed aristocracy. There was enough wealth and influence amongst the citizens of York to raise many splendid new structures such as John Shaw who built himself a fine house close to Minster Yard in 1725. Many medieval buildings were demolished or adapted to new needs such as John Wolstenholme's shop at the corner of Minster Gates which had new shop windows installed. In 1740 the York County Hospital was built, the only purpose built hospital in the north of England at the time.

The suburbs of York began to expand outside the City walls along Bootham, Monkgate and Blossom St. At first the buildings were fine townhouses with spacious gardens and later terraces of houses for working people. Despite the best efforts of the City Council, traffic congestion grew and by 1763 an Act of Parliament was necessary for the 'Better Cleaning and Enlightening the Streets, Lanes and Publick Ways of the City of York and the Suburbs thereof …and for the keeping the same in Repair and Free from Annoyance; and for the regulating the Hackney Coachmen and Chairmen, Carmen and Draymen.' By the end of the century York was cleaner and more organised than ever in its history.

The demands of the aristocracy and the export trade meant that many York merchants flourished. Butter from the surrounding countryside was exported in large quantities and the Quaker Tuke family imported tea, coffee and chocolate and began the association of York with chocolate manufacture by the Rowntree family. Others manufactured combs, which became very fashionable with the new hairstyles and newspapers and printers flourished. John Hinxman published the first two volumes of Laurence Sterne's *Tristram Shandy* in 1759.

The old trades continued. There were 16 breweries in the city as well as bakers, cobblers and tanners who worked at riverside sites outside the city walls. The regular markets brought fresh food from the surrounding countryside.

Transport in and out of the city improved with the building of turnpike roads and the journey time from York to London by coach was cut from fours days to 36 hours. Improvements in the navigability of the river Ouse as well as the improved roads maintained York's position as a regional supplier of quality merchandise.

It is reckoned that by the end of the century one third of York's population of 17,000 formed the wealthiest level of society and a half was engaged in supplying goods and services to them. The remaining sizeable minority lived in poverty. The Corporation provided relief to the poor in times of hardship either by providing work or the supply of basic essentials and in 1768 a Union Workhouse was established for 150 paupers. The wealthy of the city left charitable bequests or established almshouses such as Wandesford House in Bootham. Those who slipped through this net congregated in old and decrepit buildings around Walmgate, Gillygate and Water Lanes.

The eighteenth century was a time of elegance and growth for York but the next century, with its Industrial Revolution was to challenge the importance of the city as never before.

Lord Rockingham

Lord Rockingham is an example of the wealthy aristocrats who patronised York in the eighteenth century. His country estate was near Malton in the North Riding but he used York as his power base. In 1753 the Rockingham Club was formed in the city to promote his political career and he became leader of the Whig Party and Prime Minister Twice in 1765 and 1782.

YORK IN THE NINETEENTH CENTURY

Above Precentor's Court

The nineteenth century is seen as a time of growth, innovation and rapid social and economic changes. All of these factors effected York to a greater or lesser extent.

The outline of the medieval city was still intact with the skyline dominated by the Minster and the parish churches. The walls were still there, despite attempts in the 1820s to have them pulled down and many of the streets had hardly altered their appearance from the medieval Shambles to the splendid Georgian houses lining the better streets of the city. But beneath this familiar surface, the city was changing.

New streets had appeared. In 1836 Parliament Street was created out of a dense mass of buildings between Thursday Market and Pavement and St Leonard's Place, George Hudson Street, Clifford Street and Duncombe Place were all created at this time. The Old Ouse bridge from 1566 was replaced in 1820 and two new bridges across the river were built by 1881. By 1877 a new railway station was in place outside the walls to replace the temporary one constructed in Tanner Row in 1841.

Right
York's first railway station

Between 1801 and 1901 the population of York trebled from 16,846 to 54,742 and York's boundaries were extended to take in surrounding suburban villages raising the population of this 'Greater York' to 83,058 by 1901. As in times past, the majority of the new population were drawn in from the surrounding countryside where the population of some villages declined, although newcomers came from as far away as Ireland with nearly two thousand Irish-born citizens in York in 1851.

This rapid growth in population meant a growth in the built up area of the city as new housing and industrial sites were needed. At the beginning of the century, York had hardly moved beyond its Medieval walls with much open space within the walls but the 1849 Ordnance Survey map of York shows the beginning of developments outside the walls and by 1901 this development had accelerated so that within the walls there was hardly any open spaces and beyond the walls rows of houses and industrial sites had filled in all the gaps and were stretching out to the surrounding villages.

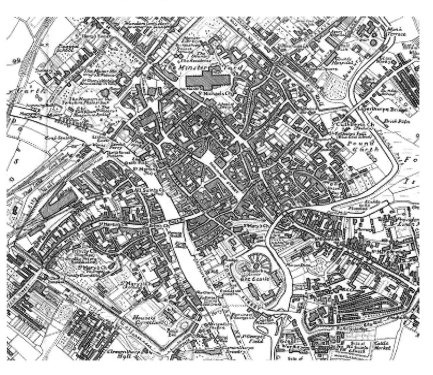

Above
The Ordnance
Survey map of York
in 1849

Despite some small scale manufacturing such as iron, glass and printing, York can hardly be said to have taken a full part in the manufacturing revolution which was transforming other Yorkshire cities such as Hull and Leeds. The majority of its citizens still earned their living in the service industries such as banking and insurance and in small-scale handicraft industries and shop-keeping for men and domestic service for women. The fairs and markets still flourished with the fortnightly cattle market growing to such an extent that a new site had to be found for it outside Walmgate Bar. Pigs were still sold every week near Foss Bridge.

Before the coming of the railway, York depended on the main coach routes to London and north to Newcastle with heavy goods relying on water transport. Boats of 150 tons could still use the lower Ouse from York and smaller boats could head north to Ripon and Boroughbridge with coal being brought in from the West Riding by barge.

The railways came to York in 1839 with a link to Leeds and Selby and by 1840 it was possible to travel to London via Derby. Driven by the York entrepreneur, George Hudson, new lines spread to the outlying towns and when several railway companies amalgamated to form the North Eastern Railway, York was chosen as its headquarters. By the end of the century the railway industry employed 5,500 workers in York making it the city's biggest single employer. The effects on road and water transport were almost immediate with the last mail coach leaving York in 1842 and traffic on the Ouse declining by a third by 1844.

Below
Rowntree Advert

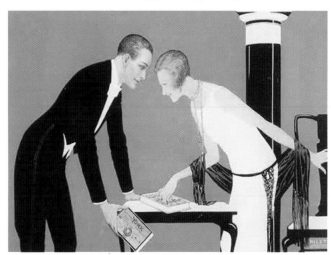

The greatest manufacturing success story in York was the confectionary and cocoa trade begun by Joseph Terry in 1838 and Thomas Craven and culminating in the international success of the Quaker Rowntree family with its well known brands of fruit gums and Kit-Kat bars. By 1908 the Rowntree works moved from North Street to a new factory on the Haxby Road employing 3,000 workers and making it York's second biggest employer.

The government of the city was still in the hands of the Corporation which was self-elected, its members remaining in office until they died. The Corporation's responsibilities were mainly the administration of justice and the maintenance of roads and public buildings and the Ouse Navigation. The poor were looked after by the individual parishes until these responsibilities were taken over by the York Poor Law Union. The corporation suffered from a lack of finance, being unable to charge rates on the citizens and inefficiency bordering on corruption when it spent £2,742 on a new banqueting house, for the exclusive use of the Corporation, at Naburn Lock at a time when the river itself was silting up.

Policing and paving of the city were taken over by an Improvement Commission in 1825 and by 1835 the Corporation was reformed by Act of Parliament. Now councillors were to be elected and the forty-eight councillors were to meet together in one chamber to administer the city. By 1879 the new Corporation was responsible for public health, the fire brigade, trams and policing as well as many of its old responsibilities. Water, gas and electric supplies were still in the hands of private companies until the corporation took over the responsibility for electric supply in 1901 with just 180 consumers.

York continued to send two members to Parliament in the nineteenth century, almost always a Whig and a Tory, later a Liberal and a Conservative and drawn from a small number of families such as the Leemans and Milners. The corporation was dominated by the Liberals until the late 1880s when the Conservatives came to power and retained control until 1945. One Labour councillor, James O'Connor, was elected in 1893.

The growing population generated a spate of church and chapel building in the city. The Church of England suffered from old and dank churches but reacted by refurbishing some and building new where it could. The new religions could start from scratch and the Methodists, who were the second largest group, began a building programme culminating in the Centenary Chapel in St Saviourgate which could hold 1,500 people. Other smaller groups such as the Baptists and Salvation Army added to the growth in places of worship. With a growing Irish population, the Catholic Church built St George's off Walmgate in 1850 and St Wilfrid's was rebuilt in 1864 with a tower designed so that it appeared bigger than those of the Minster whose services attracted only around fifty worshipers. Aware that many of York's poor were reluctant to step inside the churches and chapels, 'mission rooms' were established, such as that at Hungate in 1861, to take the Christian message out more directly.

Below
Methodist
Central Chapel

York had a long tradition of education stretching back to Alcuin in the eighth century. Ancient schools such as St Peter's adapted and changed over the centuries to ensure their survival, serving the children of the middle-classes. In comparison to many other towns and cities, the young people of York were comparatively well served by the educational establishments and it has been estimated that by 1836, about two thirds of all children between the ages of five and fifteen were receiving some kind of education. The sons and daughters of the rich were still educated privately at home but the middle classes had a variety of schools established for their children, often attached to or supported by religious denominations. The Quakers established a girls' school in 1813 and one for boys in 1827 and similar establishments were founded by the Wesleyans and Catholics. Education for the poor was not so substantial, relying largely on Sunday schools run by the Anglican National Society and small schools attached to specific churches such as those at St Cuthberts. Nevertheless, when the 1870 Education Act allowed for the building of schools, 'where none existed', there was no need to build further schools and it was not until 1889 that a School Board built six new elementary schools in York. To help staff the elementary schools, St John's College began training teachers in 1841 and by 1913 numbers had risen to 120. The city had to wait until 1902 until central government thought it necessary to provide free secondary education leading on to University entrance.

Despite these many improvements, the lot of the poor in York was still desperate. In the poor working class areas the smell of human excrement and animal dung was overpowering. Overcrowding was endemic with families living in one room and the average life expectancy in the poorest parishes near the river being only twenty years. Many families still fetched their water from the river where raw sewage was emptied or from shallow wells. Not surprisingly York suffered from two outbreaks of cholera in 1832 and 1849 and a typhus epidemic in 1849 which killed in all 1040 people. The 1848 Public Health Act led to the creation of the York Board of Health in 1850 but this body only spent £8,519 on sewerage over six years and most of that in middle class areas which needed it least. The death rate was actually increasing in York towards the end of the century with one in three children failing to reach their fifth birthday. This despite reasonable hospital provision at York County Hospital and the York Dispensary.

In 1899 a report by Benjamin Rowntree showed that over 3,000 working-class families were living in conditions which had not changed since the beginning of the century.

Above
Children going to work

For those not ground down by poverty, the nineteenth century saw an expansion of leisure time activities. For the respectable working classes there was the public house with its warmth and music, brass bands, often formed at the place of work and sport with York Cricket Club dating back to 1784, 'York Amateurs', a rugby union team from 1868 and York City Football Club formed in 1908. For the middle classes and the dwindling number of aristocrats there was the racing, theatre, music and clubs, libraries, Mechanics Institute and museums. In 1879 an Exhibition Hall was opened in Exhibition Square with a display of Fine Arts and Industry. The building was later sold to the Corporation to become the City Art Gallery.

Left Art Gallery

For the majority, life in York had become more pleasant and vibrant during the nineteenth century but for a substantial underclass life was as degrading and wretched as ever.

George Hudson

George Hudson was born in Howsham near York in 1800. He set up trade as a linen-draper in York and in 1828 he inherited £30,000. This allowed him to enter politics and he was three times Lord Mayor of York and in 1845 MP for Sunderland. His nickname, the 'Railway King' comes from his involvement in the North Midland Railway in which he was a heavy investor. In the boom of 1847 – 48 he pushed through rapid expansion of the local railways with lines stretching out from York to almost every town and village. His enemies accused him of illegal practices and of 'cooking' the company's books and legal proceedings stripped him of most of his wealth. He continued as an MP until 1859 and died in 1871.

YORK IN THE TWENTIETH CENTURY

Anyone born in York in 1900 would have been born into a world of horses rather than cars, letters rather than email and a rare trip on the railway to one of the seaside towns rather than a flight to Spain or Australia for a holiday. To say that the twentieth century has been 'a century of change' is to state the obvious for all centuries have brought about their changes. What is special about the twentieth century is the rate of change. From the Wright brothers first powered flight in 1903 to the landing on the moon was just sixty-three years. From the Boer War of 1902 when the British Empire was at its height to the signing of the documents which gave the UK entry into the European Union was just seventy-one years and from the first secondary schools provided by the state in 1902 to the establishment of a University in York, just sixty years. All in the lifetime of one person.

The story of the City of York in the twentieth century mirrored the rate of change for the individual. It has had to adapt and respond to the new challenges while looking for a new role for itself.

In 1900 York was still largely a commercial city, providing employment for its inhabitants in the chocolate factories and the railways as well as a host of small enterprises from printing to glass works. Its service industries such as banking and insurance and its many shops served not only the citizens of York but much of the surrounding countryside. But all was not well in York and in 1901 Seebohm Rowntree's book, *Poverty: A Study of Town Life* not only surveyed the poor of York but analysed the reasons for poverty and hence had a wider national importance. York was no better and no worse than many towns and cities in England but Rowntree's findings still shocked and roused many. Rowntree reckoned that only 12% of York's working population were well housed and some 10% lived below the basic poverty line, which he had formulated.

The problem of decent housing was tackled at a private and public level. The Rowntree family purchased land near its factory and built the model village of New Earswick with a theatre, Folk Hall and library as well as dwellings surrounded by gardens and allotments. The 1909 and 1919 Housing and Town Planning Acts allowed the Corporation to finance the demolition of slums and the building of council houses. About 450 of the worst houses in the Walmgate area were knocked down and the

Below New Earswick Social Housing

inhabitants moved to the new Tang Hall and Acomb estates. Private development was encouraged. Between 1919 and 1939 nearly 2,000 houses were demolished and 7,000 people re-housed removing the worst of York's slums.

York's association with the armed services is attested by the extensive Fulford Barracks which has housed many units of the army, most notably the Prince of Wales Own Regiment of Yorkshire which distinguished itself at the battle of Imphal in Burma. York itself was hardly touched by the two world wars although it was bombed in both conflicts, some 87 inhabitants being killed and the ancient Guildhall and railway station destroyed in 1942. The surrounding airfields were more obvious targets. The many citizens of York who gave their lives in defence of their country in the two world wars are commemorated by the city's war memorial in Station Road, dedicated in 1925.

Left War Memorial

York's population was growing. In 1901 it had been 77,914; by 1931 it was 84,813 by 1961 106,000 and in 2001 174,400. This pressure on space was largely overcome by the outward spread of the city. The temptation to demolish the old and build high-rise blocks which now disfigure so many other cities, was considered and, thankfully, rejected by Bill Burke, Chairman of the Housing Committee who declared: 'Over my dead body will we have bloody tower blocks in York.' York has remained largely at street level with nothing higher than the nave of the Minster.

If York's citizens were better housed, its economic base was still dependent on its two main industries, chocolate and the railways. By 1939, 30% of York's working population worked in the confectionary industry and 13% for the railways. This narrow economic

The Minster from the City Walls, York.

Above
Wall and Minster 1907

base was recognised as early as 1907 when the Corporation set up a committee to encourage new industries to come to York, which had some success. The British Sugar Corporation set up in Acomb in 1927 and the printing industry was employing 1,000 people by 1929. This was enough to see York through the worst of the depression of the 1930s but this only put the problem off. By 2006, only Nestlés were manufacturing confectionary in York, the railway's carriageworks had closed, as had the sugar works and only 11% of the population earned their living in manufacturing as opposed to the 44% who worked in finance and 33% in the tourist and retail sector. These figures tell the story of the post-war years in York which had transformed itself from a place in which to make and distribute goods to a place to visit as a tourist or to go shopping or sell insurance and software from off a computer screen.

York Shopping

This gentrification of the workplace was to be reflected in York's housing. Riverside warehouses were converted into smart flats and 'executive homes' and flats were constructed by local builders as spaces became available. The forced selling of council houses by the Thatcher government in 1979 meant that the building of affordable housing was given over to the York Housing Association and despite their efforts, young people have found it increasingly difficult to get on the housing ladder as house prices have spiralled, fuelled by the growing number of students looking to rent a place while in York. Many now commute in from Selby and other surrounding towns and villages where housing is cheaper.

Right Riverside Flats

Increased affluence meant that the motorcar threatened to choke York's streets, never meant for such numbers. At first the policy was to accommodate the car with a ring of car parks around the city centre within a short walking distance of the shops. Those not intending to stay but travel through were shunted round an inner ring road, following the city walls and later an outer ring road for through traffic. As the congestion increased, visitors were encouraged to 'park and ride', to leave their cars at sites outside the city and take a bus in to the centre. The centre itself was closed to traffic after ten o'clock making it pedestrian friendly. Bike lanes have encouraged the return of the bike, which used to be ubiquitous in the city.

One result of this policy has been the siting of many large stores off the ring road so that shoppers with cars do not need to go into the centre at all. Many inner city shops, unable to compete have closed, undermining the drive to get people to live in the city centre. Old buildings have taken on new forms. Banks have become coffee houses, gentlemen's clubs pizza restaurants.

York is rich in museums from the Castle Museum, Yorkshire Museum and Fairfax House to the newly created National Railway Museum and Jorvik Viking Museum, the visitor is spoilt for choice.

Religion has lost its central place in York's life. Despite its new charismatic Archbishop, John Sentamu, the Minster is a place to visit rather than worship in, as are many of the remaining churches, chapels and meeting houses. Only 6% of the population now worship regularly on a Sunday and the average age of these is rising. Many of the churches, which became redundant as people turned away from organised religion, have found new uses such as day centres, museums and, most successfully, the National Early Music Centre, the fate of St Margaret's in Walmgate.

The leisure industry has grown and changed to attract the new clientele. City centre bars and clubs stay open longer, spilling their raucous drinkers on to the pavements late at night. Cinemas have moved to the outskirts in large multi-screen complexes while York's two theatres cater for middle-brow, middle England.

Television remains the biggest entertainer with the average citizen now spending nearly four hours a day watching the set with its bewildering number of channels beamed in from satelites. For those prepared to leave the comfort of their centrally heated living rooms, York still offers a variety of sports to watch or take part in and clubs and societies to join, from the York Light Operatic Society to the Shotokan Karate Club.

As if to remind the City of its place in a fragile ecosystem, two natural disasters struck York at the end of the century. In 1984 the Minster was struck by lightning, causing extensive damage to the South Transept but allowing some fresh designs by young people including a whale and an astronaut now looking down from the ceiling. Then in the year 2000 heavy rains caused the Ouse to spill its banks flooding large areas of the city and bringing Prime Minister Blair to wade through the waters around Clifford's Tower.

Below
Tony Blair sees
York floods in 2000

The problems outlined by Rowntree at the beginning of the century have largely disappeared to be replaced by others. York remains a beautiful and vibrant place in which to live and work and to visit. The balance between visitor and resident is a delicate one, the income and jobs brought in by the former is perhaps worth the sacrifice of relatively high prices of goods in the shops and expensive housing. The city will never recover its former industrial base but has transformed itself into a lively tourist and service city in the same way it did in the eighteenth century when the cloth trade declined.

When King George VI visited York in 1923 he proclaimed that 'The history of York is the history of England'. This book has outlined the continuity of the city's 2,000 year history from Roman to Modern and shown how with public and private planning and foresight, a city can reform and rejuvenate itself to the benefit of resident and visitor.

Seebohm Rowntree

Seebohm Rowntree was born in York in 1871 and became chairman of the family chocolate firm in 1925, a post he held until 1941. Inspired by his Quaker faith and socialist beliefs, he used the wealth created by the firm to fund studies of social problems and to better the lives of his workers and the citizens of York by building a model village at New Earswick. He died in 1954.

Further Reading

The History of York by Patrick Nuttgens, Blackthorn Press, 2001
Marston Moor by PR Newman and PR Roberts, Blackthorn Press, 2003

Acknowledgements

The Blackthorn Press acknowledges and thanks the following for their kind assistance in providing photographs and drawings:

English Heritage; Museo Thyssen-Bornemisza; York Archaeological Trust; City of York Museums; Patrick Nuttgens; Mary Evans Picture Library; York Evening Press; Roy Burrell; Jackie Stonehouse; George Morrow; Fine Art Photograph Library; The Dean & Chapter of York Minster.

All photographs are by the author.